W9-DAX-750

WITHDRAWN

How To Convince Your Parents You Can...

Care For A Pet Hedgehog

Tammy Gagne

Mitchell Lane
PUBLISHERS

P.O. Box 196
Hockessin, Delaware 19707
Visit us on the web: www.mitchelllane.com
Comments? email us: mitchelllane@mitchelllane.com

Mitchell Lane
PUBLISHERS

Copyright © 2010 by Mitchell Lane Publishers. All rights reserved. No part of this book may be reproduced without written permission from the publisher. Printed and bound in the United States of America.

Printing   1   2   3   4   5   6   7   8   9

A Robbie Reader/How to Convince Your Parents You Can...

Care for a Kitten	Care for a Pet Mouse
Care for a Pet Bunny	Care for a Pet Parrot
Care for a Pet Chameleon	Care for a Pet Racing Pigeon
Care for a Pet Chimpanzee	Care for a Pet Snake
Care for a Pet Chinchilla	Care for a Pet Sugar Glider
Care for a Pet Ferret	Care for a Pet Tarantula
Care for a Pet Guinea Pig	Care for a Pet Wolfdog
Care for a Pet Hamster	Care for a Potbellied Pig
Care for a Pet Hedgehog	Care for a Puppy
Care for a Pet Horse	Care for a Wild Chincoteague Pony

Library of Congress Cataloging-in-Publication Data
Gagne, Tammy.
  Care for a pet hedgehog / by Tammy Gagne.
      p. cm. — (A Robbie reader. How to convince your parents you can...)
  Includes bibliographical references and index.
  ISBN 978-1-58415-798-4 (library bound)
  1. Hedgehogs as pets—Juvenile literature. I. Title. II. Title: How to convince your parents you can—care for a pet hedgehog.
  SF459.H43G34 2010
  636.9'332—dc22
                                                                                2009027349

ABOUT THE AUTHOR: Tammy Gagne is a freelance writer who specializes in the health and behavior of companion animals. She is the author of numerous books for both adults and children, including *How to Convince Your Parents You Can Care for a Pet Wolfdog* and *How to Convince Your Parents You Can Care for a Pet Racing Pigeon*. She lives in northern New England with her husband, son, dogs, and parrots.

PUBLISHER'S NOTE: The facts on which this story is based have been thoroughly researched. Documentation of such research is listed on page 30. While every possible effort has been made to ensure accuracy, the publisher will not assume liability for damages caused by inaccuracies in the data, and makes no warranty on the accuracy of the information contained herein.
                                                                                PLB

TABLE OF CONTENTS

Words in **bold** type can be found in the glossary.

Although you and your hedgehog may get off to a prickly start, your spiny companion will grow more relaxed as you love and care for it.

  Chapter One

GO HEDGEHOG WILD

"What is that?" your friends may ask when they first see your pet hedgehog. "It looks like a tiny porcupine!" Hedgehogs do indeed remind many people of porcupines. Like porcupines, hedgehogs are covered with spines, also called quills. Yet the two species are not related. Hedgehogs are related to moles and shrews.

Hedgehogs can make fun pets for the right people. Because they are so small, you can take hedgehogs almost anywhere. They are not the most social pets, though. When they see strangers, most hedgehogs curl up into balls to protect themselves. Many squeal when they are especially frightened. But these behaviors usually just make people want to know more about these interesting little creatures.

In the popular videogame series *Sonic the Hedgehog*, Sonic's best friend is a fox. In real life your hedgehog probably won't get along this well with other animals. In the wild, hedgehogs are lone creatures. Most cats and dogs, however, can be taught to live peacefully around hedgehogs. Once these bigger animals have been poked by a hedgehog spine, they quickly realize that chasing these prickly animals just isn't worth the game.

Hedgehogs are **nocturnal** (nok-TUR-nul). This means they sleep during the day. They are alert and active at night. This trait makes the hedgehog a great pet for children, since kids are in school most days. By the time your hedgehog is waking up, you will be home to care for and play with this pet.

Hedgehogs use their bodies to express their feelings. This form of communication is called **body language**. When a hedgehog's spines lie flat, you know the animal is feeling relaxed. When a hedgehog raises its spines, then the animal is feeling uneasy about something. If a hedgehog raises only certain spines, whatever is bothering your pet is likely in that direction.

Parents may worry that you could be hurt by your hedgehog's quills. It is true that a hedgehog can injure the hand holding it. Once you learn how to properly pick up this animal, though, your risk of being pricked is small. This is especially true once you and your pet have gotten to know each other. The good news is that hedgehogs do not throw their quills.

Convincing your parents that you can care for a pet hedgehog is not an impossible task. But it may take some effort on your behalf. Hedgehogs are fairly easy to own, but like all animals, they need regular care and attention. You must be sure you are ready for a hedgehog before you ask for one.

Most parents know little about hedgehogs. It is up to you to learn as much as you can about them and share the information with your mother and father. By doing this, you will encourage them to say yes to your request. If your parents see that you have done your research, they may be more comfortable with the idea of buying you this pet.

Wild hedgehogs sleep in small burrows or nests of grass.

Chapter Two

LEARNING MORE ABOUT HEDGEHOGS

Wild hedgehogs live in Europe, Asia, and Africa. They can be found in woods, gardens, and farmlands. In many countries, laws protect hedgehogs from being trapped and kept as pets. No wild hedgehogs live in North America.

Hedgehogs are **insectivores** (in-SEK-tih-voors). This means they eat insects. Insectivores have been around for millions of years. In fact, the ancestors of today's hedgehogs lived on the earth 100 million years ago. They walked the earth at the time of the dinosaurs.

Hedgehogs have long, pointed snouts and very small eyes. Most wild species have five toes on each of their four feet. Hedgehogs can have up to 36 teeth in their tiny mouths. The body parts an insectivore uses most are its ears and nose. Hedgehogs use their sharp hearing and sense of smell to find food at night.

In addition to insects, wild hedgehogs eat frogs and toads, worms and caterpillars, and small birds. Some will even eat small snakes. Most hedgehogs love eggs. They will steal eggs right out of birds' nests. They will also eat many fruits and vegetables.

funFACTS

During hibernation, a hedgehog's body temperature drops to match the temperature of its surroundings.

From April to September, female hedgehogs have litters of babies. A hedgehog can have a single baby or as many as ten in one litter. The babies are called **hoglets**. When the hoglets are born, their spines are under their skin. The spines grow within a day. At first they are soft, but they soon harden to help protect the animals from enemies.

From November until March, wild hedgehogs **hibernate** (HY-ber-nayt). This means they go into a deep sleep. They make nests out of dry leaves and twigs, usually under bushes or logs. Hedgehogs eat as much as they can before this time. They can live off the fat in their bodies while they hibernate. On warmer days, hedgehogs awaken to eat and drink if necessary.

Wild hedgehogs usually live about two to three years. Pet hedgehogs can live much longer. They don't

Hedgehogs are born with their spines just under their skin. The spines emerge around 36 hours after birth.

have to worry about **predators** (PREH-duh-turs), such as badgers, owls, and foxes. You can expect your pet to live as long as ten years if you take good care of it.

The most common hedgehog species seen in the United States is the white-bellied hedgehog (*Atelerix albiventris*). It is also called the African Pygmy hedgehog or the four-toed hedgehog. This animal will grow to about six to nine inches (15 to 23 cm) long. You may have to look closely to see it, but an adult hedgehog also has a tail that is about a half inch (1 cm) long. Most hedgehogs weigh between 11 and

20 ounces (¼ to ¾ kilograms). This is about half the size of an adult guinea pig.

White-bellied hedgehogs have **agouti** (uh-GOO-tee) spines, which means they are striped with more than one color. Most are brown and cream. Other color patterns are salt-and-pepper (black and white), cinnamon, and snowflake (mostly white).

The spines lie on the upper half of the hedgehog's body. Its face, belly, and legs are covered with soft fur. It can use its strong circle of muscles

When a hedgehog rolls up, its spines protect its face and soft underbelly.

Hedgehogs make many sounds to communicate. A happy hedgehog will gently purr or snuffle. Hedgehogs that feel threatened will hiss. Puffing or snorting means the hedgehog is uncomfortable or nervous. If it is in pain, frightened, or upset, a hedgehog will scream.

under its loose skin to pull itself into a grapefruit-sized ball, which makes the spines poke out.

Most hedgehogs have very sweet personalities. Males and females make equally good pets. Once your hedgehog gets to know you, it will raise its quills less often. Many pet hedgehogs sit with their spines flat, waiting for their owners to pick them up and play with them.

An average hedgehog has about 5,000 spines on its body.

FINDING A HEDGEHOG

The best place to buy a hedgehog is from a breeder. Search the Internet or your local yellow pages for a breeder in your area. Good breeders strive to produce healthy hedgehogs. They also welcome visits from their customers. You can find hedgehogs in some pet shops, but it is not recommended that you buy one from there.

A healthy hedgehog has eyes that are large, dark, and shiny. Its nose should be moist, not dry and not runny. A healthy hedgehog also has no lice, fleas, or ticks in its fur. If a hedgehog looks healthy, next check its cage. Is it clean? Is it warm enough? The answers to both questions should be yes.

A tame hedgehog will make a much better pet than one that is extremely shy or fearful of people. Good breeders handle their hedgehogs every day to help ensure good personalities. You will pay more for these friendly pets, but this is money worth spending.

Make sure your hedgehog is at least eight weeks old when you bring it home. In many areas, hedgehogs as young as four to six weeks can be sold. But these young animals are probably not ready to leave their mothers. If you take them before this time, you may have a number of problems with them. They may not **bond** with you properly, and they may even become sick.

Once you have chosen your hedgehog, you will need to purchase a few supplies. Every hedgehog needs a warm place to sleep. This means you must buy your pet a cage and place a sleeping box inside it. The cage should be at least 2 square feet (2 feet by 1 foot, for example). Some breeders recommend the cage be no less than 4 square feet (such as 2 feet by 2 feet). The cage should have a solid floor; the floor should not be made of wire.

Fill both the cage and the box with a soft bedding material. Corncob bedding or pine shavings usually work best. A heat lamp and a thermometer will help you make sure your pet's home is the right temperature. Try to keep it between 70°F and 85°F (21°C and 29°C). Your hedgehog also will need a food bowl and a water bottle.

Feed your hedgehog pellets made specifically for this species. These can be purchased at many pet supply stores. Pellets alone are not enough, however. You should also feed your pet hedgehog small

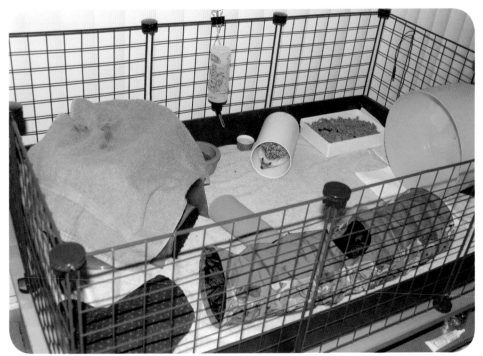

A hedgehog's cage should have enough room for it to move around and also places for it to hide. Because hedgehogs are natural burrowers, they enjoy concealing themselves inside play tunnels and under old towels.

amounts of fresh meat, fruit, live or freeze-dried insects, and mealworms.

Begin by purchasing just one hedgehog. If you are able to convince your parents to buy you a second hedgehog in the future, it will need its own cage. It will also need the same amount of care and attention as your first pet.

Until you are used to dealing with your hedgehog's spines, it may be wise to use a towel or blanket when handling your pet.

Chapter Four 4

CARING FOR A HEDGEHOG

The best time to feed your hedgehog is around six o'clock in the evening. Hedgehogs that are properly fed do not devour their food as soon as it is put in front of them. Check your pet's dish before you go to bed. If the bowl is empty, add a bit more food then. This too will probably be gone by morning.

Hedgehogs need regular exercise. Keeping an exercise wheel in your pet's cage is a smart idea. But hedgehogs also need to move around outside their cages. Fortunately, you can take your pet for a long *walk* right inside your home. This makes caring for a hedgehog easy, even on rainy days.

You must keep your hedgehog safe when it roams outside its cage. If there are other animals in your home, never leave them alone with your hedgehog. If your other pets scare your hedgehog, it is best to keep them in another room. Be sure to tell all your family members before you take your pet out of its cage. A person can accidentally step on a hedgehog or even close it in a door.

If you have a fenced backyard, bring your hedgehog outside on sunny days. Your pet will delight in running around, exploring, and hunting for insects. Never leave your hedgehog alone outdoors, though.

Keeping your hedgehog clean is a simple task. Simply wash its cage every few days, and provide fresh bedding material. Your hedgehog will do the rest. Hedgehogs are very neat animals. They groom themselves regularly.

You will need to bathe your pet once or twice each year. Simply place your hedgehog in about two

The best time to trim your hedgehog's nails is after a bath. The water will soften your pet's nails and make cutting them easier.

inches (5 cm) of lukewarm water and carefully wash it with a flea shampoo made for dogs or cats. You should wear gloves while bathing your pet so that your pet's quills don't prick you. Unfortunately, many hedgehogs detest baths.

Nail trimming is another task most hedgehogs dislike. If your pet gets outside regularly, you may not have to perform this task at all. Ask your vet to check your pet's nails at each checkup.

*fun*FACTS

Hedgehogs do not go through a shedding season. They lose just a few spines each week or two. If your hedgehog loses any more than this at once, seek veterinary care.

Handling a hedgehog can be painful if you do not know how to do it properly. Does this mean you must use gloves when handling your pet? Most of the time, the answer is no. Using gloves may even keep your pet from being able to recognize you. Hedgehogs rely on their sense of smell, and gloves can mask your scent. You may get pricked once or twice, but you shouldn't end up in the emergency room. Wash your hands right away to avoid irritation.

Begin by letting your hedgehog sniff your hand. Then gently place one hand under your pet. Cup your other hand over your pet to hold the animal steady before lifting.

If you have trouble lifting your hedgehog when you first bring it home, try using a kitchen spoon or spatula. Once your pet is used to you, this shouldn't be necessary any longer. Also, avoid handling your hedgehog during the day. Sleepy hedgehogs can be very grumpy. Wash your hands after handling your hedgehog.

Hedgehogs occasionally perform a ritual called **anointing** (uh-NOINT-ing). When the animal comes across a new scent, it will lick and bite the source. It will then form a scented froth in its mouth and paste it on its spines with its tongue.

Your hedgehog will be fine home alone when you go to school. You can even leave your pet if you go away for one night. Just be sure it has enough food and water before you leave. If you go on vacation, you will need to ask a friend to care for your pet while you are gone. Ideally this should be someone who already knows how to care for hedgehogs.

Not every animal doctor is skilled with hedgehogs. Ask around to see if an **exotics veterinarian** (ek-ZAH-tiks veh-truh-NAYR-ee-un) near you will be able to treat your animal. You should take your pet to the vet at least once a year for a checkup. You will need to make additional visits to the vet if your pet is injured or if you notice any signs of illness. It is very important that a sick hedgehog is brought to a vet as soon as possible. Your pet needs to see a vet if it vomits, limps, or refuses to eat for more than two nights.

The American Academy of Pediatrics recommends that children be at least five years old before owning a hedgehog. Hedgehogs can be dangerous for younger kids, because their quills can penetrate skin and spread a germ that can cause fever, stomach pain, and a rash. Hedgehogs may also carry Salmonella and cause ringworm and other diseases. Young children can catch these diseases more easily than older kids can. Younger kids also tend to put their fingers in their mouths often. Always wash your hands after handling any pet.

Chapter Five

BEFORE MAKING UP YOUR MIND

Before you present your case to your parents, you must decide if a hedgehog is indeed the right pet for you. Remember, this isn't a pet that will give you kisses like a dog or a cat. Hedgehogs can bond with their owners, but they do not show affection like many other pets.

Is it legal to own a hedgehog where you live? Find the answer to this question before you take any more steps.

Will you be bothered by your hedgehog's diet? Feeding pellets or fruit is easy, but will you be able to handle offering it live food? A healthy hedgehog should be fed both insects and mealworms.

These little animals live a long time. Are you prepared to care for a hedgehog for the next ten years? You must be certain you won't become bored with your hedgehog. Once you commit to owning your pet, it will depend on you for the rest of its life.

It is important to remember that real hedgehogs have very different personalities than the cartoon hedgehogs you may have seen in video games.

Also, who will pay for your hedgehog? Prices can vary depending on where you live, but you can expect to pay between $100 and $200 for your pet. Someone will need to buy the hedgehog, its cage, and all its other supplies. These include food and bedding material, which are ongoing costs. Your pet will also need to visit a vet at least once a year. Will you be able to help pay for any of these things?

funFACTS

Compared to many other pets, hedgehogs are relatively inexpensive to keep. Because they are so small, they don't eat much. The most expensive items you will need—a cage and the hedgehog itself—only need to be purchased once.

If you still think a hedgehog is the pet for you, now is the time to ask your parents about it. Tell them what you have already learned, and ask them to help you learn more. Many breeders have websites that list details about the hedgehogs they currently have for sale. Some even post tips for caring for this unique animal.

If you find a breeder in your area, ask to schedule a visit. Hold a hedgehog. Play with one. Do you enjoy

It is legal to own hedgehogs in most U.S. states. Before buying one, though, check with your local police department to make sure hedgehogs are allowed as pets in your area.

You may be able to find a hedgehog at your local animal shelter. If there are none available at the moment, leave your name and number in case one is surrendered. You can also search the Internet for rescued hedgehogs in need of new homes.

them just as much up close as you do when you read about them? What do your parents think of them?

If you and your parents are ready to own a hedgehog, you will have many years of fun with your little pet. If your parents say no, though, ask them if they would reconsider when you are a little older. Perhaps they think you need a bit more time before you are ready to care for this pet. By accepting their decision, you will show them just how mature you already are. This could increase your chances of getting that *yes* later.

FIND OUT MORE

Books
Leach, Michael. *Animal Neighbours: Hedgehog.* London: Hodder & Stoughton, 2005.

Works Consulted
Associated Press. "Kids Want a Hamster? Ask Your Doctor First: Pediatricians Warn about Health Risks from Unusual Pets." *MSNBC,* October 7, 2008. http://www.msnbc.msn.com/id/27035470/

International Hedgehog Association—http://hedgehogclub.com/index.html

Pavia, Audrey. *The Guide to Owning a Hedgehog.* Neptune, NJ: TFH Publications, 2003.

Vriends, Matthew M., Ph.D. and Heming-Vriends, Tanya. *Hedgehogs: A Complete Pet Owner's Manual.* New York: Barron's Educational Series, 2000.

Wrobel, Dawn. *The Hedgehog: An Owner's Guide to a Happy, Healthy Pet.* Hoboken, N.J.: Howell Book House, 1997.

On the Internet
African Pygmy Hedgehogs by Vickie
http://hedgehogsbyvickie.com/
Hedgehog Health
http://www.animalhospitals-usa.com/small_pets/hedgehog_health.html
Hedgehog World
http://www.hedgehogworld.com/
International Hedgehog Association
http://hedgehogclub.com/index.html

GLOSSARY

agouti (uh-GOO-tee)—A striped spine pattern found in hedgehogs.

anointing (uh-NOINT-ing)—A ritual performed by hedgehogs in which they lick and bite the source of new scents and spread them across their spines.

body language (BOD-ee LANG-gwij)—A form of communication in which the body is used to express feelings.

bond—To develop a close relationship.

exotics veterinarian (ek-ZAH-tiks veh-truh-NAYR-ee-un)—A doctor who treats unusual animals, like hedgehogs.

hibernate (HY-ber-nayt)—To spend the winter sleeping.

hoglet (HAWG-let)—A baby hedgehog.

insectivores (in-SEK-tih-voors)—Animals that eat insects.

nocturnal (nok-TUR-nul)—Active at night and asleep during the day.

predator (PREH-dur-tur)—An animal that hunts other animals for food.

INDEX